Lessons Learned From the Men in My Life

By
Sandie Barrie

Dedication

To All My Men

AJ

AJ, this book is for you. I wanted you to know the men in my life. These men have blessed my life. These are ordinary men doing extraordinary things in their daily lives. They are Nobel Prize winners in the game of life.

You probably will not be able to understand much of the book until you are older. But, I would like you to grow up reading the stories of the men in my life.

As I look around and see all the pressures that a little man has to deal with, I wanted you to understand there are options. I wondered who your role models would be and thought I want AJ to know these men. AJ, I want you to see the important characteristics of these men through my eyes.

These men are not perfect. They do have faults. However, in each man, you will find qualities and virtues that I prized. These qualities, I believe are the underpinnings of humanity and what brings stability to our family and the world.

The stories are not made up, the perceptions are what I see, when I think about the men in my life.

Grandma, 2010

Come join me. . .

The vignettes that follow are intended mainly for AJ to read as he grows up and learns about his family and the people that made a difference in my life. My soul is screaming to share these stories with AJ and the men that I write about in this book. I want AJ to know that as the world is changing, the men that I write about here help bring stability to it.

AJ is my first grandson. This book is also written for any other grandsons that may come to me and for all the sons of the men that are included in this book. Boys and young men take the time to read and think about the characteristics that you will see in the group of men in this book.

I do not intend to dwell on the faults of these men. Just know that they all had things that they could have done differently. They had slips and they made mistakes. They all would admit that they are not perfect. Well maybe one or two would smile and say that they were perfect, you know how men are . . .

If you are one of the men I write about be sure to talk to your children and grandchildren about the qualities and virtues written about in these pages. Be sure to explain to them why you did what you did.

Table of Winners

My Brothers

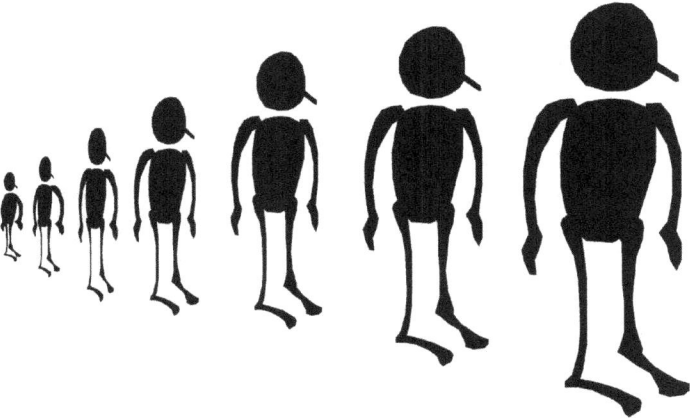

Great Uncle Richie

Great Uncle Richie is 11 months and 10 days younger than I am. We met when Mom brought Great Uncle Richie home. I cannot remember his arrival, but I am sure it was fun. AJ, for 20 days a year from February 8th to February 28th Richie and I are the same age.

We grew up together. We rode tricycles together. We played in the mud by the picnic table. We hoed the weeds, walked in the woods, and went ice-skating together. We played with Radar, the black and white cocker spaniel. We started our lives in the house, just three rooms, on the Iroquois River.

Each year another child came to play with us and each year we looked forward to the arrival of our next brother or sister. It started early on as we tried to guess if the new baby was going to be a girl or a boy. Over time, it turned into a friendly family competition between "the girls" and "the boys", each side hoping that the next child would add to their side. Eventually, we had enough brothers and sisters to be able to play softball in our front yard.

Great Uncle Richie loved to hunt and he started his adventure early in life at the side of our Dad. I never went on the hunting junkets. Great Uncle Richie loved to hunt and then he learned how to cook the treasured prize that he caught.

AJ, you can learn many things from Great Uncle Richie. I remember when he went away to college and learned all about plants and how to grow them. When he came back home, he married, and had two children. When he divorced his first wife, he made sure his two children had their father's attention.

Years later, he married again, and gained another daughter. His step-daughter had a terrible motorcycle accident. I admired how attentive Great Uncle Richie was to his step-daughter, who had significant injuries. He took the time to be with her, take her to doctor appointments, and he made sure she had what she needed to live her life as best she could.

Great Uncle Richie is a quiet guy, until he gets roused up by a card game with his brothers and then its every guy for himself. For many years, Great Uncle Richie went to visit his ailing mother-in-law. He brought her flowers from his garden and listened to her stories.

Great Uncle Richie spends quality time with his wife, making sure she has everything done that needs to be done to keep their home filled with the love they share. He is attentive to his children and his grandchildren.

When Great Uncle Richie meets God, they will be like old friends sharing stories about the beginning and the end of life. They will share stories about growing plants, swimming in the water, and raising children.

They will talk easily about women and what a good job Great Uncle Richie did at making sure that the women in his life were treated with dignity and respect. Great Uncle Richie has always had time for me. AJ, Great Uncle Richie was my first brother, from him you can learn to always have time for your sister, Emily.

Great Uncle Tommy

You have two great uncles with the name Tom. The first Great Uncle Tommy is my brother. The other is your Grandpa's brother. I know our family is so big you wonder if you will ever get them all straight. Don't worry your Dad is still trying.

My brother, your Great Uncle Tommy, likes to build things. He is a carpenter. He knows everything there is to know about hanging drywall. Great Uncle Tommy and his crews have put up many of the walls in Northern

Illinois.

Great Uncle Tommy is a real beacon in the dark. His life has been filled with events that have been most painful. I really don't want to focus on the difficulties Great Uncle Tommy has experienced, let's just say they have been unusual, hard, devastating, and fatiguing. Through all the trials and tribulations, I would like to focus on his sense of humor.

Great Uncle Tommy knows how to laugh, has a keen sense of humor, and an outrageously beautiful smile that he utilizes. Great Uncle Tommy enters the conversation, listens, and within minutes, he is cracking a group of words that has everyone in his environment laughing.

Great Uncle Tommy has a genuine smile, the kind that goes from one ear to the other and pours out through his eyes. Great Uncle Tommy's front tooth was knocked out. But, that did not make a difference, he still smiled. His muscles were trained.

Great UncleTommy lives one day at a time. I love to get a call from him because he calls me "Strawberry". When he says "Strawberry" the tone of his golden voice rings with a smile and within minutes, I am laughing. I know my brother with the smile is calling.

AJ, life has a way of getting hard in spots. Remember your Great Uncle Tommy. His way of dealing with hardships was to find a light side. By smiling and laughing, and smiling some more, he made life easier for the rest of us. There were time when we just wanted to cry as we listened to the pain and the suffering. But, how could you cry when Great Uncle Tommy was cracking a joke and laughing?

God joins in Great Uncle Tommy's every joke and laugh. God taught us that no matter how hard life got that He was walking by his side. And, God took every step with Great Uncle Tommy as they walked on the road to Heaven. When Great Uncle Tommy's soul goes to Heaven, he will be at peace with his big family because they each have learned that no matter how tough life gets, one can still smile and laugh. AJ, from Great Uncle Tommy, you can learn to make Emily laugh for the rest of your lives.

AJ, crack a group of words that make others laugh, like Great Uncle Tommy!

Great Uncle Jas

AJ, Great Uncle Jas is a quiet man with a dry sense of humor but when you listen closely, you can hear his intelligence. He is a deep thinker with a quick wit. He listens closely. And, when he is right, he is right! When he was a little boy, he liked to play board games and he liked to make up the rules, but then I liked to set-up the rules as well. Great Uncle Jas is a study in rules.

When he breaks the rules, there is a good reason, and the reason is thought out well in advance.

AJ, from Great Uncle Jas, you can learn how to reason why you are doing things differently before you act. Great Uncle Jas has always been able to explain his actions. He is not impulsive, but reasoned. He is disciplined and he expected discipline from those around him.

AJ, from Great Uncle Jas, you can learn to exercise, learn to do Tai Chi, a science of disciplined exercise. AJ spend time like Great Uncle Jas has in investing in your health, stay lean like him, walk tall, and hold your head high through the trials of life.

When Great Uncle Jas gets to Heaven, God will welcome him because Great Uncle Jas took the time to make room in his life for children who had a hard life. He made life happier for two little ones but more than that, he stayed by their side, as they developed into adults, even when life got tough.

God will lay his hand on Great Uncle Jas's shoulder, looking at His watch, telling Great Uncle Jas that he spent a lot of time, a lot of time working with His children. AJ, from Great Uncle Jas you can learn how to be a person of values that trusts their decisions. AJ, from Great Uncle Jas, you can learn always to be ready to play a game of cards with Emily.

Great Uncle Steve

Great Uncle Steve likes to be out in the country. He likes to be outdoors. He enjoys hunting.

Patience and the ability to negotiate tough situations are the hallmarks of Great Uncle Steve. When your Great Grandpa, my Papa, went to Heaven, it was Great Uncle Steve and Great Uncle Richie who straightened out the mess. Great Uncle Steve is a gentle but firm man. He has an uncanny way of listening to all sides.

Can you imagine taking the wide and varied opinions of six brothers and six sisters into consideration as you try to ferret out the land holdings of your father? Great Uncle Steve did it with grace. I never saw him lose his temper or express negative emotion at the burden he had.

Our father had asked him to do it and you know what he just did it. He worked with the lawyers, the rest of the family, and he told each of us what needed to happen and when it needed to happen. He gently took charge and made a painful process easier for the rest of us. When it was over, he still held the respect of all of us.

He held our family together with his skill. He did not let us feud. He helped each of us work through our pain by listening. He knew when to call a family meeting.

AJ, as you grow older, life will cross you with challenges. When things get tough, remember Great Uncle Steve's way of gently taking steps to bring about consensus taking into consideration the needs of others.

During the four years that it took to settle your Great Grandpa's estate, Great Uncle Steve had other challenges that belonged to his own family circle. He balanced his responsibilities to his wife, sons, and grandchildren with the responsibilities to his family of birth and to his extended family of workers.

When life seems to get out of balance, think about Great Uncle Steve and take a lesson at patience and negotiation. Be slow in your determination, be thoughtful of others, and trust that God will help you. No doubt in my mind, God has negotiated a place for Great Uncle Steve in Heaven because he knows how to fit people together. Great Uncle Steve's soul will transcend the hours of negotiating knowing that his life made a difference. AJ, from Great Uncle Steve, you can learn about listening before talking. AJ, you can learn always to be ready to listen to Emily.

Negotiating peace takes time, Bringing peace to others is calming to the soul, Helping others is an art, Cultivating the art makes a man!

Great Uncle Willie

Great Uncle Willie spent a lot of time in life listening to others, not talking much, but he knew how to be present when Papa needed him. Great Uncle Willie is a quiet and gentle man. Great Uncle Willie has a deep and genuine strength that is much deeper than the muscles of other men.

Great Uncle Willie can fix anything on a big 18 wheeler's engine. He goes to work day after day at the same location along Highway 57. The truckers depend on Great Uncle Willie to keep their engines running. Great Uncle Willie loved dogs, lots of dogs.

Great Uncle Willie enjoyed all the hours he spent raising dogs for others to enjoy. AJ, I know that you got scared by a dog in the park when you were young.

Great Uncle Willie would want you to let go of that fear.

Great Uncle Willie was one of my brothers, who spent time with our Dad in his later years. He is the one that made sure that Papa was cared for from one day to the next over many years. He went on errands for Papa and he saw that the grass around the house was cut. He brought him food cooked by his wife.

When Great Uncle Willie goes to Heaven, all the dogs God sent to him will be wagging their tails and barking wanting one more bone. God will be pleased with Great Uncle Willie because he was determined to care for those he loved. He was determined to fix the engines of the trucks that brought needed goods to market. AJ, from Great Uncle Willie, you can learn about deciding on doing something and then just doing it, even when it is the same thing day after day. AJ, you can learn from Great Uncle Willie to be always ready to help Emily.

Great Uncle Greg

Great Uncle Greg is one of my younger brothers. His nickname when he was a child was "Sheriff". Your Great Grandpa liked to give all of his children nicknames.

Great Uncle Greg was so much fun when he was a child. He and Great Uncle Terry were always trying to get me to give them snacks from the refrigerator.

Great Uncle Greg is my tallest brother and he has the most hair. When he was growing up, he had much fun that sometimes landed him in trying to explain to our Mom, what he had done.

Great Uncle Greg loves to hunt, as many of my brothers like to do. Great Uncle Greg loves to play cards and talks just a little louder than the rest of the men. He offers ideas that make sense. He spent his life raising his daughter. He lived in trailers and many different houses. After Papa died, he stayed in our family home until decisions about it could be made.

Great Uncle Greg gave up alcohol when he determined that it was not good for him. He spends time learning about good health habits.

Great Uncle Greg knows a lot about cars. One day when he came out to Sparks to visit me, we went and looked at old cars. I learned that he once painted cars for a living, which I never knew.

When Great Uncle Greg goes to Heaven, God will be proud to welcome Great Uncle Greg because he took steps to take care of Papa and his daughter. He responded to needs and helped many men out as they struggled with their alcohol problems. AJ, from Great Uncle Greg, you can learn to be patient with yourself as you grow into becoming a man. AJ, from Great Uncle Greg, you can learn always to have patience with Emily.

Great Uncle Terry

Great Uncle Terry is my baby brother. I still remember the day when my Aunt Dorothy called at our home, when the phone hung on the wall by the fireplace, and told me how lucky we were we didn't lose our Mom when Great Uncle Terry was born. I was all of 13.

I remember Great Uncle Terry when he was a little boy, he was always so much fun. He loved to run around the house and play with his toys.

Great Uncle Terry went off to college and became a banker. Great Uncle Terry married and had a couple of kids. Great Uncle Terry liked his big garden.

Great Uncle Terry took the lead when the family decided to sell the family farm. He made wise choices, as we had several complexities, that had to be handled. He helped us all understand what needed to be done.

When God welcomes Great Uncle Terry into Heaven, He will be especially proud of the work Great Uncle Terry did with all the people who needed loans to buy property.

Great Uncle Terry is a patient man who uses his intelligence to help others. AJ, from Great Uncle Terry, learn early on how to handle money and use your money wisely to serve your needs and the needs of others. AJ, from Great Uncle Terry, you can learn always to be ready to help Emily with the decisions that need to be made in life.

My Brother-in-Laws

Great Uncle Kenny

It is easy to write about Great Uncle Kenny. Great Uncle Kenny is Grandpa's brother. He is a very religious person, but not in the "academic" way. He doesn't preach it, he lives it, and then lets the kids in his life watch him. In addition, it was not just for one ballgame or one group of kids. No! it was for hundreds of kids, one year after the other, for all of his married life.

AJ, think turquoise that is glistening with the shine of hope. See a beautiful wide smile. Then visualize a house located in St. Anne, IL where all kids are welcome and where there have been hundreds of parties for kids with no alcohol.

Great Uncle Kenny grew up on a farm. He worked hard. He married a generous woman and together they forged a relationship to give of themselves to children who lived in Northern Illinois.

While Great Uncle Kenny had many health issues, that didn't stop him from giving to others. He never spent a day without helping someone else who needed his help whether it be finding a postal code; to helping children understand why their parents were doing what they were doing; to tending to Uncle Chuck and Aunt Dorothy in their final days, before they went to Heaven.

Great Uncle Kenny was just there for his kids and thousands of other kids who needed his help.

Great Uncle Kenny taught me how to put aside anxieties about my health and to live life while I waited to go to Heaven. I have always known that Uncle Kenny would find a big comfortable chair next to God because God gave him several special assignments that he handled with gusto. AJ, you would be well served to go to one of Uncle Kenny's Friday night parties where you truly can learn to have fun from a man who never lost his love for children!

Great Uncle Charlie

Now in a book like this you are not suppose to have favorites, it is not politically correct so just let me say, I love to be in Great Uncle Charlie's presence. Great Uncle Charlie is Grandpa's brother.

He is a big man; He has a chest and shoulder on him that demonstrates to the world that he is a man, a man's man. He understands what it is like to get dirty with the dirt of the fields. He understands cold and hot. He understands what it means to work long days, to keep the farm equipment running, and to help the other farmers. He knows about bug bites.

When I think of color with Great Uncle Charlie, I kind of smile, wondering what he would look like in purple? I got to watch him grow up from a little guy. I was there the day that he cried at Great Grandpa's funeral. He tills the ground and with Great Uncle Donnie, he raises crops of corn and soybeans, that start the food chain that feeds the rest of the world.

Great Uncle Charlie likes toy tractors and tractor shows. Great Uncle Charlie stops what he is doing whenever somebody needs him. He helps the other farmers, many of them old. He helps the farmers' widows. He cared for his Mom. He watches over his wife and children like a hawk. He drives the school bus. In addition, there is one thing for sure, when Great Uncle Charlie says to get in your seat, it doesn't have to be said twice.

He is a big teddy bear, gentle, gentle, very gentle. However, his gentleness should not be confused with quietness. He is not quiet, what you can learn from him is to speak up for what you value, that is, to stand tall, to have an opinion and to voice that opinion.

Great Uncle Charlie will not have any problem fitting into God's plan for him to join Him in Heaven. The angels will be clapping their hands when Great Uncle Charlie walks through the gates and his warm smile will fill the glow. The angels will be clapping for a man who had values, lived those values, and by example taught them to others. AJ, remember always the fun time you had driving Uncle Charlie's tractor!

Great Uncle Tom

Remember, I told you that you have two Great Uncles with the name Tom. Well let me tell you about Great Uncle Tom, who is your Grandpa's brother.

One day in life, you will need to confront a tough situation. Great Uncle Tom worked at the same institution that I worked at when I first became a nurse. Great Uncle Tom worked as a security guard. It was his job to make sure residents, who were mentally retarded, stayed safe during his watch.

He was responsible to care for those who could not care for themselves. He treated each individual with respect as he helped him or her settle their bodies down so that they did not get hurt or they did not hurt someone else. It was not an easy job, but one that Great Uncle Tom did with calmness and grace.

Great Uncle Tom loved animals; he cared for horses. He made the horses happy as he brushed their hair; cleaned their space; and loaded and unloaded them into trailers so that others could see their beauty.

Great Uncle Tom gave many hours of service to helping farm the fields with his brothers. He gave much of his time to others. He was a tender quiet man who spent his hours providing guidance to all his children. Great Uncle Tom juggled his life responsibilities with tact. He knew when to say something and when to keep quiet.

Great Uncle Tom will ride into Heaven on a gorgeous

horse! God will be pleased with all the time he spent patiently grooming the horses. The animals in Heaven will run to Great Uncle Tom knowing that he will always do the extra task to keep them comfortable. AJ, from Great Uncle Tom, you can learn how to love animals. On your next trip to Illinois, be sure to visit his coral and take a ride on one of his horses!

Great Uncle Donnie

Great Uncle Donnie likes tractors, little toy tractors. He collects them. At one time, these tractors lined the kitchen of his mother's home, lined up in perfect order. Great Uncle Donnie is your Grandpa's brother.

Great Uncle Donnie drives a bus and farms. Great Uncle Donnie was the last one in your Grandpa's family to leave home and to marry. He farmed the land but he also tended to the routine of an elderly woman. He stayed at home and spent the time carrying for his Mom, your Great Grandma.

I have watched Great Uncle Donnie grow-up from a small child to a truly stellar example of a man. He quietly did whatever needed to be done. He just did it, whatever his Mom needed to have done. AJ, in Great Uncle Donnie, you have an example of what the word generosity means.

For Great Uncle Donnie the time he spent was time that he wanted to spend. Great Uncle Donnie has a presence about him that every man should learn. He would come into his Mom's room, sit, and talk to her. He tended to her personnel needs. He did not gripe about what he did. Great Uncle Donnie drove her to the doctor appointments and stayed with her in the hospital.

AJ, I can't explain to you how much I appreciate what I saw in Great Uncle Donnie's respect for his mother and the commitment he made to her in her later years.

Great Uncle Donnie allowed his Mom the privilege to stay in the farmhouse through many years of illness because he saw to it that she had food and heat and medicine.

God will welcome Great Uncle Donnie into Heaven because Great Uncle Donnie understood generosity of personal time. Great Uncle Donnie demonstrated to his Mom repeatedly that she was the most important person in his life. Great Uncle Donnie taught us all how to patiently sit by those we love. He spent his time with her. In return, God will make time for Great Uncle Donnie and sit with him at a table filled with kindness, hope, and love.

AJ, from Great Uncle Donnie, you can learn how to sit quietly and give support to those who need your attention. You can learn about making someone else's needs more important than your own needs. AJ, you can learn how to share time from Great Uncle Donnie. AJ, I know that you love to go outdoors, be sure to take time in life to visit Great Uncle Donnie's farms often!

Life is how we spend our time! Spend it wisely!

Great Uncle Jerry

Great Uncle Jerry is married to my sister, Ronnie. They married many years ago. AJ, you can learn two valuable lessons from Great Uncle Jerry: one is financial and the other is spiritual. Great Uncle Jerry learned early the value of money, how to use money and how to "sock it away". Great Uncle Jerry had many jobs working for large companies and has flown all over the world.

Great Uncle Jerry wore a corporate suit and he also wore the garb of a deacon. Great Uncle Jerry moved his family to several locations around the USA and even to Canada. Great Uncle Jerry was in a position where he made decisions that effected many people's jobs, a position that he took very seriously, one that he handled with grace and dignity.

AJ, from Great Uncle Jerry, you can learn it is not about the house one lives in, but the relationship building within the family, no matter which house they lived in that makes a difference! Great Uncle Jerry made sure that each family member had a special spot.

AJ, Great Uncle Jerry has a sacredness about him that walks a very special line between being in the corporate life and his precious family and his church responsibilities.

AJ, you can learn from Great Uncle Jerry about allowing your family to banter about their ideas and about what they think about issues. You can learn to enjoy meals with your family to come and to encourage them to listen to each other. Freedom of speech and thought were always permitted at Great Uncle Jerry's dinner table, not only permitted but encouraged.

AJ, Great Uncle Jerry had a lot of financial resources, and he worked hard to balance the financial resources with the spiritual resources. He spent hours of time helping those in need to learn both about financial and spiritual issues.

AJ, Great Uncle Jerry's mind was always busy trying to help someone fix something. God will welcome Great Uncle Jerry into Heaven wearing his deacon robes. They will talk easily about the homilies he gave at countless Masses that helped others gain a different perspective about life. From Great Uncle Jerry, you can learn how to set goals for yourself and reach out and work at obtaining them. AJ, be sure to catch up with Great Uncle Jerry, I am sure he has two books he wants you to read, one that teaches you about finances and one that teaches you about spirituality!

Great Uncle Mike

Great Uncle Mike is married to my sister, Ginger. They married many years ago. Of all of the men in this book, I don't know Great Uncle Mike very well. His path and mine have not crossed many times.

AJ, over the years I have learned about Great Uncle Mike, from my sister as she talks about him often with great affection. AJ, I do know that Great Uncle Mike has worked hard as a nurse. Being a nurse, Great Uncle Mike has tended to the needs of many old men, many of them military men. AJ, Great Uncle Mike has a solitary way about himself that is not always understood by others.

Great Uncle Mike chose a quiet life where he went to work, and came home, and went to work, and came home. Great Uncle Mike suffered many problems but never gave up with trying to figure out how to cope. AJ, from Great Uncle Mike, you can learn how to keep trying when life becomes difficult.

When Great Uncle Mike enters Heaven, God will reward him with many kind words for taking care of others while he was on Earth. From Great Uncle Mike, you

can learn how to share your time with those who are
ill and help them feel better physically and mentally.
From Great Uncle Mike, you can learn how to live life
in a way that makes the lives of others a little more
comfortable. I am sure Great Uncle Mike would have
a story or two about how to deal with pain, and how to
relieve pain so that people do not have to suffer!

Great Uncle Terry

Great Uncle Terry is married to my sister, Jean. They
married many years ago. Great Uncle Terry was an only
child, that is until he met my sister and then our family
engulfed him and made our family his family. Great
Uncle Terry learned his role as brother-in-law easily; he
loved parties and always fit into the family parties. All
were happy when Great Uncle Terry joined the party.
He made any family gathering a little more special when
he was there.

When one is an only child, as was Great Uncle Terry,
you have extra responsibilities when it comes to caring
for your parents as they become older. Day after day
after day, Great Uncle Terry made sure that first his
Mom and then his Dad were cared for as their bodies
and their minds tired prior to their trips to Heaven.

Great Uncle Terry bought many pieces of real estate
and with my sister they fixed the properties up so that
other people would have a place to stay in an Illinois
college town.

Great Uncle Terry had a great sense for letting people
around him do what they wanted to do. He encouraged
his wife and daughter to do those things in life that
made them happy. AJ, from Great Uncle Terry, you can
learn about happiness, you can learn how to make other
people smile.

AJ, I am sure that Great Uncle Terry would love to

take you to New Orleans. He loved to go there, listen to the music, and eat the great food. He loved adventures like you do. When God welcomes Great Uncle Terry into Heaven, He will have a smile on His face. Listen to Great Uncle Terry carefully for he is skilled in knowing how to talk about something you will both enjoy!

Great Uncle Terry will know that he earned his final party place in Heaven because he helped so many others have fun, while he was on Earth. AJ, be sure to seek out Great Uncle Terry and give him a big hug like I always wanted to do. He will start to talk about something instantly you will both enjoy!

Great Uncle Roy

Great Uncle Roy is married to my sister, Angie. Great Uncle Roy enjoys the water. He spent hours giving people rides on his boat. He loves to fish. Great Uncle Roy chose to marry my sister when they were young. He spent his life providing a special place for her and their son to live.

Great Uncle Roy brought consistency to life. He stayed the course of making a home along the river, even with all of its floods. Great Uncle Roy drove many hours every day to keep his job up North, close to Chicago. He ventured out when it was very hot and very cold to make sure that he kept his job.

AJ, from Great Uncle Roy you can learn about taking the time to make sure that everything is taken care of for your family. Great Uncle Roy meticulously made sure that his family had food on the table and clothes on their back.

Great Uncle Roy took special attention with his son guiding him through boyhood into manhood. AJ, from Great Uncle Roy, you can learn to make wise decisions in life, even when you are a young man. You can learn from Great Uncle Roy to take time to make decisions to improve one's life situation.

AJ, when Great Uncle Roy, goes to Heaven, there will be a special dock where he can enjoy the pleasures of boating and fishing because he took the time to share his time with his family, when he was on Earth.

AJ, be sure to visit Great Uncle Roy and have him take you for a boat ride on the Iroquois River right by Papa's old home. He will navigate the river with ease and tell you the many stories of how it has changed with time!

My Colleagues

Dan

I met Dan on the locked men's ward at the state mental institution. He was one of the first men that I met when I walked onto the night shift, as a nurse, in the summer of 1967.

Dan wore black thick rim glasses and very white uniforms. So with Dan think "white". Dan was tall and strong. Dan and I worked side by side caring for men who were mentally ill.

Dan watched over me very carefully to make sure that I stayed safe on our tour of duty. While I worked on the wards, I was pregnant with your Dad and then Uncle Kevin. The patients were usually sleeping but sometimes they would wake up and need something to drink or had to get up to the bathroom.

Dan made sure that I didn't get hurt during the night, while we watched the patients sleep. Most nights the men were quiet and so we sat and talked. However, there were other nights when the darkness came forward from the spirit of these men. AJ, from Dan, you can learn to keep an eye on all pregnant women wherever they are.

Life is so precious, especially the beginning of life. From Dan you can learn how to be sure that woman, especially pregnant woman, are held in special esteem. Watch over them, make sure that you talk to them, give them a genuine smile, and just listen.

God will welcome Dan into Heaven as a man who spent his life caring for those who were a little bit on the edge, a little different, a little scared. He walked many of them to the bathroom. He held the cup for them to drink the water. He changed their beds. He covered their bodies and he took them to the morgue. And, he watched very closely one pregnant woman. So remember from Dan that there is great peace in knowing that you have helped someone who needs your help.

AJ, Dan will always hold a special spot in my heart because he took care of me many nights, as we watched and cared for those men in need. AJ, I am sure God will hold Dan in the palm of his hand and gently place him in Heaven with all his old friends, who lived in the mental institution. AJ, from Dan, you can learn to smile at pregnant women because they are carrying new life and they need your smile!

Ralph

Ralph was my patient. I tended to him before he died from cancer. AJ, as I start to tell you about Ralph, you might not understand why I found him to be special. When I came to the locked men's ward in the late 60's, I learned about life real fast. I had never been around people who were different. I didn't understand about mental illness. I didn't understand anything about the concept of patient's rights. But, before Ralph was my patient, Ralph was my helper, he worked for cigarettes and received them each morning from the ward staff.

And, the cigarettes ruined Ralph's body, but not his heart and soul. Ralph was a patient in the mental institution. I never really could understand why Ralph was there. He seemed very "normal". He came early around 5 AM each morning to help "special" the patients. "Specialing" was the term used to move from bed to bed; clean the patient; put on dry clothes; straighten or change the linen; pull up the side-rails; and offer them a drink of water. The process started with running water into a large pan, stacking sheets, and blankets on the old but stable table, and then rolling the table from bed to bed.

Many beds filled the ward. The space was divided into rooms separated by half-walls, with six beds in each space, that provided no privacy. Many patients could no longer get up. Therefore, they were "specialed" every couple of hours.

AJ, from Ralph my colleague, you can learn how to tend to the sick and the dying. Ralph came into the ward from his ward where he was housed, each morning to help me get the patients up. He was old but he still could work, work for the cigarettes. In those days, there were no rules about patient's working. No one thought it hurt the patients if they did something for their keep, while they stayed in the big institution.

AJ, from Ralph, you can learn real humility. He did the things that no one else in society would do. He took care of human beings that no one wanted. He was gentle with them. I never asked why Ralph was in the mental institution. He seemed so normal.

It was a quiet night that night Ralph died and I stood on his right side, near his bed. I felt like I had lost more than a colleague, actually a friend, since he had stood by me many a morning, as we tended to the sick and the dying.

I only learned months later, after his death, the reason why Ralph was in the mental institution. Even when I found out, I really never wanted to believe what I heard. I am sure God healed his soul when he came through the gates of Heaven and told him he had done his time. AJ, from Ralph, you can learn gentleness, patience, and hope when things don't go the way you want them to go. AJ, from Ralph, you can learn how to minister to the sick and dying.

Roy

It does seem a little weird to put the words, "my black friend", after Roy's name in the poem I wrote for him. However, all the other men in this book are white, that is, Caucasian and this friend is of African American decent. Until I was 21, I never was around very many people who were different in race, culture, or religion. When I went to work with the mentally retarded children, I met Roy.

From Roy, AJ, you can learn about sharing with those who are different from you. AJ, Roy opened up my eyes, so that I could see that there were many different types of folks in this world. Yes, Roy taught me a lot about black people but that was not what was at the heart of his soul.

He taught me even more about how to work with people who were mentally challenged. He taught me how to be patient with them. He taught me the concept of active listening. AJ, active listening is very hard. It is hard not to finish the sentences of those with whom we talk and Roy liked to talk. He really liked to talk. But, he was even better at listening, especially active listening.

When Roy arrives in Heaven, I see God and Roy sitting next to each other. Roy is quietly listening to God talk about the world that He created. In listening, God will tap Roy on the shoulder and ask him for consultation on how to get the peoples of the world to listen to each other. AJ, from Roy, you can learn how to teach others to get along with people that are different from themselves. Enjoy the poem I sent to Roy, many a year ago, when Grandpa and I moved from Topeka to Sparks.

Sandie Barrie

Roy, my black friend . . .

I found him in an institution for
the mentally retarded; no! he was not
one of the lovely residents, but one
of the staff. He had a small dingy
office, lacking in most of the office
amenities.

And . . . I avoided this office across
the hall, with the quiet black man!
For . . . I was sure he would see through
me . . . and would know I was scared . . .
scared mostly of his black skin!

Slowly . . . ever so slowly, he and I
bided each other the day, and even
more slowly the smiles came. Oh, it
took time . . . A lot of time and I
can't remember now who stuck their head
first into the other office.

But as time went by, we spoke more to
each other and taught each other about
ourselves and our cultures . . . And oh,
how I learned from this black man whom
I had once feared.

Skillful he was in the art of listening
and debate . . . Some discussions went on
for months. He raised more emotion in
me . . . challenged me more . . . Caused me
really to think and certainly influenced me!!!

And, I was able to discover in the years
I knew him, a human being who gave much
of himself, whom you spoke to after 9 in
the morning, one who loved basketball, and
one who took the extra step for people . . .

Sensitive and gentle he was to me and my
needs and even now when I am 2000 miles
away I want to keep the relationship alive
. . . for he is an inspiration and a reminder
that mastery of fear brings discovery . . .

For if I had never ventured, never smiled,
never shared, I might have never learned,
as I did . . . from this relationship, that
one's own self often stifles growth and
happiness more than anything else.

Yes, he is still there giving and
sharing . . . and the world is a better
place because he stays in that little
office, available to those in need.
All I can say about him and his
way is alright . . . Alright . . . ALRIGHT!!!
Circa 1979

AJ, remember active listening only hears what one is really trying to say!

Dr. Tom

I met Dr. Tom, when I worked in the healthcare program in Kansas. Dr. Tom always had a white shirt and tie on. He wore a gold colored coat. He answered the phone and he tried to figure out how to solve problems for patients. When you think of Dr. Tom, think gold sparkling with the specks of a flashing smile.

From Dr. Tom you can learn how to get at the heart of a problem. Dr. Tom looked for details, the details that made the difference. Dr. Tom's job had him trying to grease the space between the Medicaid regulations and people who were in dire need and the doctors that were caught in the middle. Dr. Tom took his work seriously. He never shied away from confrontation. He took on the problems that no one else could handle or would handle and brought them to resolution.

When Dr. Tom worked a situation, he became like a relentless detective trying to get at all the details. He wrote voluminous notes that he referenced often as he worked at finding the turning point in each situation. He dug for each minor piece of data and wove them together like a fine piece of cloth. When he was done with his investigation, he had brought a kind and sensitive brain to bear on the controversy.

The lesson learned was persistence at getting to the truth of a situation. He didn't stop until there were answers in his mind for all the nagging questions. He challenged his own opinion forcing all to see the many sides of a conflict. When he spoke others listened because he had done his homework and often his investigation demonstrated a faulty regulation, where some physician and his patient were suffering.

From Dr. Tom take a bit of his persistence in researching out life's questions. Don't give up to easily when something doesn't seem right; just keep an open mind to the facts.

Dr. Tom was already an old man, when I met him in semi-retirement. He taught me that as humans we have the capacity to persevere until we find the answers to questions. I learned that we do not always have to take what someone tells us as the truth, and that we need to form our own opinions, after serious research.

Dr. Tom burst into Heaven where God had assembled people who did not know Dr. Tom, but whom he had helped through his interpretation of the health care rules. God told Dr. Tom that in Heaven there was not a pecking order and that all people are truly equal, which made Dr. Tom's soul shine. AJ, from Dr. Tom, you can learn how to double check your ideas to make sure you want to move forward with your decisions.

Dr. John

I worked with a lot of doctors since I was a nurse for a long time. When I think back over all the healing men I worked with, one sticks out in my mind. He was even my boss for a short time. AJ, from Dr. John, there are many things that you can learn. But, one important lesson is the telling of stories. When you think of Dr. John, think of blue water, calming water settling in a pond.

Dr. John was a respected and loved physician that had the privilege of standing on the shoulders of his peers to look out to see what was coming. He then was able to look them in the eye and give them the story "straight", as they needed to hear it, but in a very gentle way.

His words were smooth, elegant, and calm. He had a way of delivering "news" that allowed one to hear it without any biases. He was a humble man!

Dr. John gave me a blue vase for Valentine's Day one year, filled with beautiful pink and blue flowers, the year he decided to retire. AJ, you have seen the prized blue vase in my collection of precious objects in the big family room. AJ, when Dr. John retired from his job, I had the privilege of being with him in a large room filled with lots of doctors and nurses and friends. Below are the words I wrote for him and shared with his colleagues. There was not a dry eye in the room.

AJ, relish for a few minutes the images of Dr. John, as he went through his busy days as the chief medical officer in a large urban hospital.

Remembering Dr. John

- Walking down the hallway in a hurry to one more meeting;

- Sitting at your desk with your hand to your forehead not making eye contact, just thinking;

- Stopping the discussion with a great story that illustrates the point beautifully;

- Stating four sentences, as you rush by in the hallway that made our day;

- Smiling and then laughing and then laughing some more;

- Never saying no, just modifying the idea slightly;

- Standing at the intersection of the cafeteria hall and the gift shop talking to everyone who came by;

- Knowing the brother of the patient, or the father of the patient, or the whole patient's family, or the patient, during the administrative review of patients on Tuesday;

- Everyone wanting you to be on their committee;

- Sitting with a family making a difficult decision about stopping the machines;

- Checking things out with your great friend Helen over and over and over and over;

- Holding the door, holding the chair, shaking hands, smiling;

- Signing papers and more papers and more papers;

- Negotiating with the case managers over and over and over;

- Meeting with doctors and nurses and Bonne;

- Going into Medical Staff Services and getting something good to eat;

- Sitting at the Nugget Christmas Party with your beautiful wife, Eileen;

- Singing Silent Night at the Employee Christmas Party;

- Helping, helping and helping, making a connection here and there that made everyone's job easier;

- Explaining to Bill why things were going so well or needed slight adjustment;

- Checking with Beverly for messages or your schedule;

- Adding your clinical expertise to cases where your ideas made a difference . . . a big difference;

- Remembering ideas that everyone else had forgotten;

- Sitting at the Board meetings interjecting the answer to a tough question eloquently;

- Seeing the answer . . .

- Being a gentle man . . .

- Being a patient man . . .

- Being a kind man . . .

- Being a wise man . . .

- Being a loving man . . .

- Being yourself . . . a man of personal integrity and dignity.

Circa 1996

When Dr. John crawled into Heaven, God was there to heal his pain and to make his soul whole. Dr. John's soul jumped for joy with the other souls he had helped on their way to Heaven. He rejoiced in the peace knowing that he had walked through life sharing the oath, "To do no harm".

AJ, from Dr. John, learn how to frame your words so that others will want to listen to what you have to say.

AJ, try not to do any harm as you move through life.

Dr. Tom

A second Dr. Tom entered my life. He worked at the hospital in Reno, Nevada. He had spent most of his years in the lab, studying slides and diagnosing diseases. When he decided to retire, he became my boss.

From him AJ, you can learn how to do things in order, how to transition from one phase of life to the next. In addition, you can learn that men sometimes change their minds.

I had to meet with Dr. Tom on a weekly basis to go over my work assignments. At the time, I was developing a new program that was controversial. The one thing that Dr. Tom taught me to do was to develop an agenda for those meetings. He taught me how to put things down in writing that needed discussion with him. Then he went down each item one at a time. He taught me how to look methodically at issues, before making decisions. He put some left brain into my right brain! Dr.Tom will be welcomed into Heaven because he liked order and he was compassionate.

Dr. Tom helped me leave my work when I stopped working at hospitals. He was very gentle with me. It was very hard for me to leave. AJ, from Dr. Tom, you can learn how to help your family and friends step through change that has to occur in their life.

Bob

AJ, men have come in and out of my life. I wish you could know Bob. Our time together was short. When you think of Bob think of red, the color of his chubby cheeks. He worked with me at the hospital. One day I was listening to him lecture and his words rang true for me. As a result of knowing Bob, I learned something about myself and I changed something about me.

AJ, it is important to know that you will touch other lives, even when you have no idea that you are touching their lives. On my birthday each year, I like to surprise someone with a piece, that I wrote years ago. I first wrote this piece for Great Uncle Tommy when he lost his little daughter to some strange disease when she was eight years old. For many years I gave a rendition of this piece to someone who had made a difference in my life. Bob was one of those people.

Bob is about sharing his beautiful gift of sharing his story with the world. AJ, Bob is about lighting the way for others to see, what they need to change about themselves.

When Bob meets God there will be many souls standing there watching them. And, it will be Bob's turn to watch the others who made it to Heaven because he let others watch him. Bob's soul will be at peace knowing that because he shared his life others were able to save their own soul from the fears and worries of Earth. Read the special message I did for Bob on my birthday one year, many years ago.

AJ, from Bob, you can learn that there will be people that will be watching your every step and that you will effect without your ever knowing.

Service Award Given on This 28th Day of March 1994

Bob

Service is an elusive concept. Service means different things to different folks depending on whether one is giving or receiving. For you, service is finding the inner energy within your being which allows the giving of self to others. Service is the culmination of forces deep within your soul which gives purpose to your existence.

Service requires no special education or position. The tools of service are simple: a warm smile, a kind gesture, a soft touch and a twinkling eye. Service doesn't cost a lot of money or time to provide. At times, though, it takes a lot of raw guts to face others and demonstrate service. You relish service the most when no one realizes that you have provided it. For you, service is best shown when the smoothness of delivery doesn't elicit an obligation.

Service is action, realizing something needs to be done, and doing it. Service is walking in other peoples' shoes and empathizing with their situation. Service is providing another the opportunity to make a choice and helping them to decide. Service is power in knowing you do make a difference. Service comes with the nurturing, simply put . . . the caring about another.

The beauty of service is having found your niche on earth and fulfilling your role to the best of your abilities. Service is knowing that what you are doing is important and that it must be done right. Service is stretching slowly for improvement in what you do. Service is taking the time for replenishing your inner energy resources, developing your self-esteem, and gaining the strength to look anew at each situation. Service is taking delight in the simple things of life: a bright smile, a sunny day, and a warm cup of tea.

In healing, it is the culmination of generous service, which makes the difference. The climate for renewal of body and spirit is enhanced with the time you took to demonstrate:

your ability to challenge, your factual stirring speeches, your pleasantness, your healthiness, your peaceful smile, your professional clean-cut attitude, your clear eyes, and your plain happiness in what you do. You are a great role model for other professionals. It is your personal enthusiasm for these ideals, which brings about their realization and gives life and breath to the concept of service.

In the humility of providing service to others you are made keenly aware how service is shared and the squeak is taken out of your day. You do not work alone! You do not walk alone! Know I walk with you in your work. You have made many days shine for me and for this I smile! . . . I appreciate all you did for me, much of which you will never understand . . . you helped me gain back my life. One in which, I hope I can make a difference like you have!!!

AJ, light the world for others to see!

Dr. David

You could call this vignette, "You Got Mail". I worked at getting a degree for a very long time. And, Dr. David was the man that had more faith in me than I had in myself. Right from the start, he wanted me to write for publication. I told him that I didn't think I had the time to write for publication and for school. So I chose school.

When school got tough for me and I wanted to give up on school, he just kept focusing me on to the end. He didn't give me the answers, he just asked questions. He is a military man and sometimes it felt like I was in the military with him. Dr. David gave meaning to the concepts of discipline, clarity of ideas, fluid expression, figuring it out on my own, and doing it over until it was right!

Nevertheless, 10 years later, I walked on the stage and he placed the hood on me to signify that I had made it. I could join the club. I had earned my doctorate degree.

AJ, I have only seen Dr. David three times in my life, but we have shared hundreds of emails. Moreover, in each email, he provided direction to help me on my way. When Dr. David goes on to the next world, God will understand that he didn't always know all the answers.

Nevertheless, since Dr. David encouraged others to improve, God will recognize him and let him join the club. He will not have to do orals and his papers will all be accepted because he took time with his students. AJ, remember that no matter what you have to say to do it in such a way that the receiver is left with encouragement to continue.

Father Norm

As you will find later in this book, I took the death of my father very hard. I had suffered through a serious depression and I was dragging myself out of the pit of feeling sorry for my loss, when I met Father Norm.

Father Norm is a man of the cloth, a Roman Catholic priest. He has a love for the people of God. For a long time he was involved with educating children until later in his life when he decided to finally fulfill his life-time dream of becoming a priest.

Father Norm gave me an opportunity to pull myself from the depths of hopelessness and to refocus my life after my father died. Father Norm had a bible study where he invited parishioners to come together to read, think, and provide inspiration for the following Sunday's Gospel reading and homily.

A small group came together; it was part of my healing to join this group, for a few months, at a very lonely time in my life. After we read the intended readings, something sparked in my mind. I wanted to do something about the Gospel not just read and think about what had been read.

I wanted to provide a service to others.

Father Norm suggested that I write a letter to the pastor of the church. Writing the letter, I asked the pastor if I could start a food donation at the church for people who did not have enough to eat. Well Father Norm made a suggestion that I followed through on that has resulted in thousands of pounds of food being donated to people in need. When Father Norm meets God, I am sure there will a strong hand shake.

AJ, from Father Norm, you can learn how making suggestions can help others move forward with their ideas.

Mike

It you have been reading from the beginning of this book, you know that I have been very careful not to talk about the good looks of any of these men. However, with Mike I can't help mention that he is very good looking. However, one soon gets pass that when they listen to him talk and learn about his value system. Mike is a family man, but not only for his personal family, but for the community as a whole. AJ, what you can find in Mike is a commitment to leave the Earth better because he spent time on it.

Mike has been involved in numerous helping projects but the ones I have found to be some of his top ones include his mission to eradicate smoking. AJ, I hope as you grow up, you will never allow someone to talk you into the use of cigarettes or for that matter any other drug. I know that you never knew my Papa but he was addicted to cigarettes and they ruined his life. He suffered greatly because of the addiction that he brought back from the war.

Mike does not only voice his dislike about cigarettes but he has jumped into the political quagmire with both feet. And, even with thigh-high boots on has found himself in one mess after another.

What is so exciting about Mike is to watch him weather each assault made by those who would have one believe that cigarettes are not dangerous and that they "have rights" to kill themselves. What he does so well is hold his head up high, look straight into the audience, and in a gentle but firm way tell it like it is.

What I admire the most is his tenaciousness, his calmness, his political savvy, and his ability to get others to join him in his effort to eradicate cigarettes from Northern Nevada.

AJ, watch people like Mike, they have been given many

gifts from the Maker and they choose to use those gifts for the community family. AJ, I know when Mike meets God, he will not need a grant to convince Him that there should not be any smoking in Heaven.

God is walking with Mike as he takes each step in his fight here on Earth so that the Earth that God made will become a healthier and safer place. God's hand is on Mike's shoulder walking him from an improved Earth to a smoke-free Heaven. AJ, from Mike, you can learn that cigarettes kill people. AJ, please make an early decision never to smoke cigarettes. AJ, be an advocate early in life to convince your friends not to ever smoke.

Cigarettes are like hammers and blades, they kill! Watch out for anyone that suggests you use cigarettes or any drugs. Just say NO!!!!!!!!!!!!!!!!!!!!!!!!!!!!

43

My Very Special Men

Joe

I can't write a book about the men in my life without writing about Joe. Joe was my "first love". He took me into his arms and gave me my first kiss, right there at the back door of my Mom and Dad's house, right by the garage. AJ, I never feared anything when I was with Joe. Life was so innocent and the adventures so new . . . so peaceful.

Joe is about being a kind man and having respect for young woman. Joe took me out on dates. Joe made me a pink rosary for my sixteenth birthday that I still have in my jewelry case today. Joe let all his pigs out so he could ask my brothers and me to come and catch them. My brothers caught the pigs and Joe gently kissed me. I remember how we took the bus before he could drive us, how he dressed up so carefully with even a top coat. I remember going to the "sock hops" and hoping Joe was there. Joe talked about being a priest. Joe started dating other girls. Joe went off to Vietnam.

When Joe came back from Vietnam, he called me up and we went for a car ride. We never talked about his war experience. I told him I was engaged to your Grandpa and he respected my decision. Later I heard he had gotten engaged. Joe married, and he has two kids that I have never gotten to meet. Joe worked in the factory and farmed the fields.

AJ, when you start dating I hope you treat your "dates" like Joe treated me. My Papa always liked Joe and Joe liked my Papa. My brothers still see Joe and I always fondly ask about him each time when I go home. There is always a story about whom he is helping. I remember he went to see my Papa a few times when he was old and ill. He cut firewood for him. I am sure my Papa probably teased Joe about me, just as he always teased me about Joe.

AJ, when you hold your first young woman in your arms

be sure that you act like Joe, and be a very kind young man. Kiss her once, pull back, and run to your home, kicking up your heels all the way!

Hallelujah!!

I know Joe will march into Heaven right behind God. God is proud to say he has been with Joe all the days of his life from the farm to Vietnam and back to the farm and factory. Because God was with him on all his adventures, he stayed safe. God has placed many opportunities to help others in front of Joe and Joe has stepped up to the "plate". I knew Joe when he was a young man and I will never forget how well he treated me. There is no doubt in my mind that Joe will be in Heaven, because God provides a front row seat for those who like Joe are true to their family and friends.

AJ, always treat young woman as Joe treated me with gentleness and kindness, it is a lesson to learn early in life and to keep close to your heart. The girls in your life will always remember gentle and kind acts done by you.

Sandie Barrie

Gail, Gary, Jimmy, and Jerry

AJ, these four men are about old friends and long-term marriages. I met all these men when I was a young person. I met three of them through your Grandpa.

Now they have all been waiting for me to write my first book. They are all worried what I might say about them. They are all still laughing about the night that I had to find my stove burners in the bushes in the front yard.

These men are the sunshine of my life. These four men are examples of men who have a high opinion for commitment. These men married their wives when they were young and now AJ, they are all still married 40 years later. And, hopefully they will spend many, many more years with their wives.

These men have all held jobs, took chances, and each night they came home to their wives and children. One of them worked on the farm, one drove trucks, one worked in an office, and one fixed copy machines.

These fellows all live in the Midwest. And, they symbolize the core values of America. They worked, they all worked, they all worked hard to "bring in the bacon".

God will celebrate these four coming to Heaven. As each gets there, they will join the party of men, who married once, worked at their marriages, and demonstrated to others what it meant to make a commitment to be married.

AJ, from these men, you can learn about fidelity and holding the woman you marry in high esteem for your lifetime.

48

AJ, these men, Gail, Gary, Jimmy, and Jerry, hold the key to successful marriages, they married well . . .

Nameless

AJ, in my life there were many men that I did not get to know. I was a lucky lady, there have been many men that thought they might be in love with me. But, seeing I was a married lady they decided not to interfere with my relationship with your Grandpa. AJ, being human you will understand later in life, that there are many opportunities in love and passion sometimes runs high. But, we all have to choose.

And, AJ, that is what love is really about, making decisions and living happily with our choices. AJ, you too will learn about love, choice, and decision. Over the years, I was thankful that these men respected my desire to maintain my relationship with Grandpa. I know that these men know that I deeply care for them. Mostly, I care because they chose to let me live my life with the one I chose. And, because they honored their decision to truly love those they chose. I know I will meet their souls in Heaven since God valued that they understood the concepts of respect, boundaries, and integrity.

AJ, from these men, you can learn how boundaries help one know what actions are acceptable and which actions are not acceptable when moving through the relationships of life.

We have a Deal!

Paul

AJ, I know from an early age that you always liked my brightly colored nails. While getting my nails "done" was important to me, even more important was the friendship that I developed with Paul, the manicurist.

Every two weeks for over 10 years, I spent an hour or so with Paul. Paul is a culture lesson, a listening friend and at the same time he made my hands look and feel good.

We discussed the latest movie, the latest war conflict, the latest news. We shared our inner feelings. One thing we agree on is that we should take each day for itself.

Many times I was a few minutes late for my appointments but Paul was always there waiting. Paul spent many hours with me listening to the stories of my life. He appreciated America more than most people I knew. He had to leave his home country of Vietnam during the war. He taught me the value of freedom. He taught me to appreciate that we get to say what we want, we get to walk where we want to walk, and that we have the ability to make a difference in the lives of others.

I know God will welcome Paul into Heaven where there will be no wars. He will be joined by his family who has been scattered around the world and they will talk about their adventures, how so many people seem different but how in reality they are all the same. God will welcome this tender man into Heaven to see all his customers with shiny fingernails.

AJ, from Paul you can learn humility, patience, and thankfulness that he found our homeland. He taught me to appreciate how lucky I was to be born an American. AJ, always respect the privilege of being born American, be sure never to take the privilege for granted!

Sandie Barrie

Dick

AJ, Dick is a very special friend. I count myself very lucky to have met Dick. I met Dick when I was pregnant with Uncle Chris. I remember the night. I was as big as a pregnant lady can be and Dick just asked me to dance anyway. At the time, I did not realize I would count him amongst my dearest lifelong friends.

He loves his wife and is truly a family man. When you are around Dick and Donna there is no doubt in your mind that Dick loves Donna and that Donna loves Dick. Dick treats her very special. He is not afraid to kiss her in public. He honors her opinions. He spends time with her. He buys her flowers on their anniversary because he wants to buy them. And, he buys the BIG bouquets. They are fresh and gorgeous. But AJ, it is not the flowers that make him special. What makes him a man that you can look up to is his devotion to his family.

Dick doesn't pretend to be something he isn't. He is not a rich man say like in money, but he definitely is a rich man when it comes to the real values in the world. If his wife, children, or grandchildren need something, he is there. He is just there! He fixes the cars, the cars, and the cars. He fixes their homes. He answers their questions.

He listens to everyone. He asks hard questions in a way that makes one think. In addition, he can ask the questions because he has spent a lot of time thinking about the individual. He has a keen sense of what is making one crazy, he chooses when, and how to ask questions about what is important. He doesn't pry. Moreover, he doesn't give out compliments that are not well deserved. His favorite one line is, "Take the time to smell the roses along the way".

He worked at a job that many men would not do. He

did it well and because he did it well, there were very few interruptions in the water supply because he made sure the hundreds of pumps in our town worked. He did not talk much about his work because it was not the mainstay of his life, it simply was a means to an ends. The job provided him money that allowed him to provide for his family.

While there are hundreds of things, I could share with you. The one I remember most is Dick listening to me, while my own Dad was sick and after he died. He just listened and asked questions that allowed me to talk. He just listened, listened, listened, and helped me get through what turned out to be one of the toughest times in my life.

So, Dick went to work. He respects his wife. He listens to his friends. He attends to the needs of his children and grandchildren. While he might tell you, things are much the same every day, kind of routine. Sometimes he may try to convince you he really doesn't like the routine. However, don't let him kid you he loves the routine. For in the routine he has created a family life that other people only dream will come their way.

Dick prays in a very private way. When Dick meets his Maker, he will be able to shake His hand knowing that he followed the line. Dick will thank Him for a good life. God will welcome him into Heaven slapping him on the back. God and Dick will talk very easily about the success of his life.

AJ, perhaps the things that you can learn from Dick are to smile, to get your priorities straight, and to take the time needed for family. You would be well served to watch Dick, as father and grandfather, and to know that the respect that his children and grandchildren give to him has been earned and is well deserved.

AJ, enjoy the two poems I wrote years ago for my two friends, Dick and his wife Donna nothing more needs to be said for they say it all . . .

AJ, always find time for friends and
celebrate with your friends every
opportunity you get!

Loving for Thirty Years

Love is a decision to spend a lot of time together, sharing. Love is giving and forgiving. Love is kicking back and smelling the roses.

Love is precious. It is more than sharing the same dishes, the same bed, or the same laundry detergent. Love is singing and reading together.

Love has taught you both patience, gentleness, and kindness. Touching you have given your time to each other. Love is your specialty.

Love is more than joining sperm and egg, it is giving the world three beautiful human beings. Time well spent in teaching and sharing and loving.

Love is taking each other into consideration before fulfilling your own needs. Love is food waiting to be shared with each other. Love is sacred.

Love is quiet routine, steps taken in timely order. Love drives energy into your beings and allows you to smile within each other. Love is sensitive.

Love is demonstrating that you respect each other. Love is tender. Love is what makes the world go round and you two give it an extra spin.

Love is sharing special talents, listening more than talking. Love is commingling your beings and sharing your marriage with the world.

Love is sleeping in each other's arms for thousands of hours. Love is waking in the bright early morning, knowing there is peace at least here.

Love is spending the rest of your lives together sharing yourselves . . . and God's beauty . . . loving each other.

September, 1995

Flowers and Friends

Flowers are like friends
Friends are like flowers

Flowers are soft and fragrant
Friends are warm and serene

Flowers are bright and cheery
Friends are happy and attentive

Flowers are stem and leaf
Friends are kind and generous

Flowers are fresh
Friends are unique

Flowers are promising
Friends are encouraging

Flowers are pink and yellow and fuchsia
Friends are red and white and blue

Flowers are given as a gesture
Friends are a special gift

Flowers are earth's beauty
Friends are God's smile

Flowers are love
Friends are love

Flowers are like friends
Friends are like flowers

Gramps

I don't get to see Jack your Gramps very often. I don't know him very well. But, I do know his daughter since she happens to be your Mom.

One summer, I gained a greater respect for this man as he toiled in redecorating your house. You got a new blue bedroom.

Your Gramps was a man who worked with numbers and helped many kids who did not have family to help them along the way. He spent hours and hours of time arranging appointments for children who needed a helping hand.

Gramps loved his two daughters and demonstrated to them what they should look for in the men they should marry. He is a stellar example of generosity! Gramps will be welcomed into Heaven by God where he will not have to make any arrangements for his stay. Gramps will find that all the books balance and that money is no longer needed.

AJ, remember to take time with your children like Gramps did with his children, one of which is your Mom. He is a wonderful role model of how to love woman that will be in your life.

Great Grandpa Les

AJ, every man has a Dad and your Grandpa's Dad is a very special man. He went to Heaven when Grandpa was a young man. He was a gorgeous human being. He had brilliant blue eyes and he looked a lot like your Grandpa.

I remember things about him even though it has been a long time since I have seen him physically but he remains in my heart. Every Sunday when the priest asks for us to pray, I pray for Great Grandpa Les. I remember sitting with him at the farmhouse table. He raised Angus cows and had all the meat cut up into hamburger. There was always food on his table.

I remember him at Grandpa and my wedding. AJ, he was so happy to see us get married. He just smiled all day long and danced all night. He really did like to dance.

I remember when he came to Topeka when I needed him. He dropped everything on the farm to come and help take care of Uncle Kevin and your Dad after your Grandpa had a motorcycle accident. I remember he forgot his dentures and his medicines.

I remember him at church. He liked the back row of the church. And, he went every week. You could tell that God and church going was very important to Great Grandpa Les. He really was a humble man. He was a quiet man that "did not toot his horn a lot". He was a hard working man. He farmed the land and gave the rest of the world food. He smiled. He smiled a lot. He had friends, a lot of friends.

I know that I married your Grandpa because of his Dad. You see you look at the roots and when you saw what I saw in him you just "Go for the Gold". The last time I saw Les was at the dinner table on Good Friday, April 23, 1973. He simply stood up and went to Heaven. He walked with a generous smile and I know that God and he have been watching the rest of us for many years. I know that he smiles on his sons and daughter, particularly your Grandpa, for he just kept on going and did what needed to be done to keep the farm running.

AJ, from Great Grandpa Les, you can learn to enjoy life with a big smile, while keeping your commitments.

AJ, remember as you grow up

. . .

Farmers are people who know how
to have a great time while growing food
that feeds the rest of us

. . .

Be sure to do something in your life
that helps others as much as farmers do

. . .

And while you are doing it,
be sure you smile like Great Grandpa Les

. . .

Papa

AJ, when my Papa went to the hospital for the last time, I knew it was time for him to go to Heaven. I sat quietly at the computer in my home and wrote the following. The next morning I got on an airplane and was able to be with him during his last hours. I kissed him and two days later, I read the following to those who gathered around. My Papa was a very special man in my life. Read this piece over and over and enjoy the essence of being human and being a man who earned the love and trust of his children. I know when Papa met his Maker, there was a long talk, his soul finally free of the smoke, the alcohol, and the arthritis. God and Papa talked easily about why animals were created and how much joy they brought to those who took time to be with them.

And With His Touch of Flowers . . .

A florist, thirteen children, compassion, patience, and perseverance are the themes. The main character is Pop. The story is told by me, his eldest daughter. One thing Dad taught me was that I had to do things right because there were so many others watching me. So here goes Papa, I am going to do this right too.

World War II veteran, Camel cigarettes, flowers, flowers, and flowers were his environment. I remember him swimming in the river, and trudging us all across the rising flood waters, and watching the pond. He had dogs lots of dogs. . . Radar, the cocker spaniel, and Sonar. . . and Puppy and his last dog Star. There were many others, including Murphy.

Dad had thirteen children, born in sixteen years with no twins. There was only one Mom, our Mom. Mom was very special, she died on November 1, 1986. Mom converted to Catholicism, when she married Pop in 1945. I was born in 1946 and was the start of the family. March 1st of 1994, and Dad turned 74. And, 74 years of contributions have been made. I can't speak about the first twenty-six years because I was still only a gleam in his eye.

But, I do know that he was born into a family of florists and he took over the tradition after he came back from the war. Now, there is not much to say about the war, except Dad had medals and black and white photos of his wedding to Mom. He was in his military garb and he sure was good-looking, standing tall and proud. The medals and pictures were kept in a trunk under the house and were strictly off limits to us kids. When he returned from the war, he worked with his brother Lawrence and they took up the family tradition in Kankakee. From its inception in 1870 till 1995, 125 years of business in the same town, in three different locations.

I fondly remember the store on Court Street even though it is gone now, replaced with a fancy building. Marie, an older woman worked with Dad as his helper. It was a floral shop, across from the Big Bear grocery store. In front were all the flowers and Dad had three tables in the back. I got to work there while I was growing up, after school, I tied bows and answered the phones. Dad's greatest story about me was the time when I watered all the fake flowers. When they first came out, it never occurred to me that there was anything but real flowers in Dad's shop. I only remember my Dad working with the real thing, that is, real flowers.

Now, when one works with flowers, real flowers, they don't last. But, I can tell you that the flowers my Dad arranged while I sat behind him watching were exquisite. He was a master craftsman, a true artist. He wasn't into sales and he didn't have to move flowers that were not fresh. He arranged to get them from market several times a week or cut his own from the cloth house. Often his Camel cigarette burned the top of the ribbon bolt leaving a brown mark, while Dad carefully arranged one flower after another into the bouquet.

Dad loved his customers. He knew them each by name. He knew what they liked and what they didn't like. He pleased them with his creations. Now, the bouquets were for all occasions. Red for the men, soft pastels for the ladies, delicate arrangements for the baby funerals, and bright happy bouquets for the sick room. He was a happy man while he listened to what someone needed. His creativity was elegant in being able to capture their feelings in the arrangement of flowers. No matter what they paid for the flowers, Dad added something to each one that made it special. There were no "get well soon" plastic words stuck into his arrangements. It was a colorful butterfly, a red cardinal, an extra delicate piece of ribbon, or a beer can. It was always something special for his customers . . . all who were special to him.

We never had to take money from the state for food stamps or housing. It was a different time then. Dad bought a piece of property from his brother John when he returned from the war. He cleared the woods and built a small three room house with a large, very large garden next to it. One room was brought out from the greenhouse on Jeffrey Street. Two additions were added over the years and a second bathroom, it became known as Dad's bathroom. Dad's bathroom was simple. It wasn't heated by the general system but it did provide him privacy.

His house has rung with laughter of thirteen children and their wives and husbands and their children. It is a quieter place now but watch out for Sundays. If you want to catch up with the family, you just go out to Dad's house. One by one we all check in and if not this Sunday then next. Or, we called, as I did from Nevada. The best part of Sunday afternoons was watching the glee in Dad's eyes. Euchre was the game played -- 15-2, 15-4, 15-6. It is funny, but I know in the heart of my brothers, the ones who generally played with him, while they all sipped on beers, it was important to them that Dad would win especially in the later years. But, the game was fierce and loud. The competition was hot. The challenge was on.

The girls sat on the couches and talked to each other

about their children, Dad's grandchildren. There are a lot of them no one really keeps count. The emphasis was on how each one was doing, that each one was all right, growing and developing. Each child touched by this family was loved in a very special way. Mom and Dad taught us each how to do this by their example. We didn't take lessons. We just knew about things like discipline . . . helping each other . . . love . . . respect for each other's opinion.

Dad lived in the country on the Iroquois River. The driveway from our house to the road was about two blocks long, up two hills. I remember crunching up the road through the snow, with my boots on to catch the bus. We all rode the bus to get to school. We all have different experiences. Dad worried about us waiting for the bus. He followed me up the road to the mailbox when I went to first grade, we didn't have kindergarten in those days. I guess as the story goes, that I was singing to the black birds. Dad built me a box to sit on, and later he built a little shelter by the tree with the old rusty sign that cautions, "NO TRESSPASSING".

There was not one tree but lots of trees, something like ten acres. Ten acres of walnut and oaks . . . red and orange trees, standing between the quiet winding river and the reality of the road. Dad liked to hunt and we ate every kind of wild animal one can name. We ate squirrels and rabbits and ducks. Dad fished the river with his nightlines using night crawlers, and we ate cat fish and other fish, I didn't know the names. But I do remember the delight in Dad's eyes when his nightlines produced fish and the smell while he cleaned them. Then they were either eaten or put in the freezer by Mom. Dad shot one goose each year at Thanksgiving.

Our meals were always healthy. Dad planted a garden each year. Us kids pulled the weeds and did the harvesting and Mom was in charge of freezing and canning. We snapped green beans in front of the old black and white television set. We learned to eat vegetables and to really like them without the sauces. The girls all learned how to make pies and cakes from scratch and took great pride in cutting the piece for Dad.

Dad was a patient gentle man with us. His compassion can be remembered as we each worked at gaining his attention. We were proud when we did something that pleased him there is no question. We each weighed what we did through Dad's eyes even when we didn't want to. Mom gave us a conscious; Dad gave us understanding and forgiveness. From the time we grabbed at his knee, when he returned home for supper each night, till the time we each left the house to go out in the world, to returning home on a regular basis, Dad was always there. Dad loved to listen and he listened when no one else would. He had his opinion, which he stated sometimes more vigorously than others. Each of us kids can tell a story about Pop and the influence he had on our lives. I was in healthcare because of Pop. Somehow fashion designing in Chicago for his first born, his 18 year old daughter, didn't click in his mind.

Dad's health was vigorous when he was young. He was never home in bed. He didn't believe or even consider not going into work. After all, he had a large family to support. In addition, he was a top notch provider. But, somewhere in the 70's an old war surgery, an appendectomy done in the field, flared up. It was the beginning of many many hospitalizations for Dad. Congestive heart failure and other heart and circulatory problems added to the constant pain from arthritis.

Dad did not complain about his illnesses. He always felt like he and his family had been blessed. He believed in God and he believed God had been good to him. Now the illness wore on his children before the end . . . as they waited on him. But, each one of them had a separate lesson to gain from Dad in his final days. With Dad, his final days seemed to go on and on. When one thought that surely they were at the end of watching his pain, he sprung back like one of his flowers budding for the very first time.

There is so much to capture in the life of this one man . . . love for country, laughter, generosity, gleam in his eyes . . . tenacity . . . lessons about doing what you believe in, about being yourself . . . lessons about making commitments and keeping them . . . lessons about reality and responsibility . . . lessons about giving and receiving. Lessons about serving. For Dad, it was having a large family. And, then supporting that family through all its issues, problems, growth, disappointment, and fun. There has been much pain but even more fun. Books could be written about each ones struggle. But, the endings would all be the same . . . love and respect for the Father . . . Dad . . . Pop . . . Papa . . . Franie . . .

So now, as we each move to learning how to live without Dad in the picture, without Dad watching the river and his birds and squirrels, without the familiar phone call with Papa, we have to move on. We have had the benefit of a great man in our midst. Papa was a man who taught perseverance and tried to maintain his sense of humor. He was a man who loved to tease. He never gave up his Camels.

Some people don't understand privilege. Each of Dad's thirteen children, their spouses, his grandchildren, and great grandchildren all understand what a privilege it was to be born to his union with Mom. We know it was a struggle for Dad, but even to the end he taught us to be stubborn in what it is we do with our lives. He taught us to be in control of our life even to the end. He taught us that the responsibility for our life lies with each one of us. We know that we have to maintain the property . . . the house, even with the annual flood . . . the flagpole . . . Mom's blue spruce. We know that we can always walk on that property knowing Dad is walking with us. There, we can always be at peace. There, we can go to sort out life in the solemnity of the beauty of the woods.

We can be proud of what we all did for and with Pop, making arrangements for his care; staying with him at night; doing the little tasks in the yard and house; picking up his Lotto ticket; paying his bills; getting his oxygen; setting up his schedule of care; visiting him; calling; having one more good joke for him; watching Star; mowing the lawn; and putting in the dock. Each a lesson in compassion and humility and love. We know he is in Heaven finally with Mom . . . smiling down on each of us. They are there making the nest for each one of us.

We each know now that we each have to get on with our lives. We know that that is what Dad would want us to do. The lessons have been learned. The lessons must move on. Each time anyone of us handles a flower, each time we water a plant, each time we pass a beautiful garden, we can choose to remember Dad. We know Papa added true beauty to the world with his children and with his touch of flowers. . . May 1, 1994.

Papa was a dad and a florist who sent God's creations to others

. . .

Sharing beauty, hope, and love

. . .

To all those they touched

. . .

AJ, I am sure that God welcomed my Papa into Heaven where they have been watching all of His children grown into individuals who take their responsibilities seriously, from our Papa you can learn about perseverance and commitment. AJ, from your Great Grandpa, you can learn how to take care of the responsibilities that you take on in life.

Grandpa

AJ, I met your Grandpa, when I was 16. He offered me a ride home after we had been at his cousin Judy's house. He wanted to know if I had a birthday party at my house because all my brothers and sisters were there. We dated for 5 years and we have been married for 43 years this coming June. There is so much to tell you about your Grandpa. Let me get started.

AJ, your Grandpa is a portly man, with sterling blue eyes and he has a smile that when shared embraces his whole face. When he walks into a space, you know that he is there. He commands your attention with his eyes. He is quick to ask questions to whomever he meets. He has a way of never really getting into an argument because he knows when it is best to change the subject. He is a strong man even when his back is wrenching with pain.

Your Grandpa is not a soft romantic man. Instead, he is a man of principles, a man of integrity. He is a man who has opinions that he has spent time forming. AJ, let me try to explain. Your Grandpa did not send flowers or bring candy much to express his love for me. He did not demonstrate his love in public with kisses or holding my hand. He demonstrated his love in much more principled ways.

I selected a man to share my life with that said what he believed and then took actions to demonstrate his beliefs. He believed in God. He always went to church. As a young man, he believed in his family as he worked the land after his Dad went to Heaven. He believed in work. He always held a job. He believed in human dignity. AJ, your Grandpa treated all people with respect especially older woman!

Most importantly, he believed when he chose to become a Dad that he had responsibilities to his children. He never let me down when it came to being a supportive parent. He believed that women should have the same opportunities in life as men. He hired a female as his co-pilot. More importantly, he never stood in my way in my personal development. Instead, he always said do what you want to do.

He believed in rules. He expected everyone to drive by them! AJ, your Grandpa was a very practical man. From him, I learned the value of duct tape. I learned duct tape could stop a leak in a boat. I learned that if a door does not shut, you just could take it up to the shed and cut the top inch off. I learned that you could write how to hook the VCR to the TV in permanent ink on the top of the VCR, directions never to be lost again.

Your Grandpa lived in the fast lane. He enjoyed motorcycles, boats, cars that raced, and airplanes. He is always on the move as he tries to make life for everyone in his circle of family and friends a little easier. AJ, Grandpa loved a good joke and always had one ready to share with Dick and Donna. AJ, I am glad God let your Great Grandpa live after the nasty motorcycle accident in 1972 so you could get to know him and see him play with his "choo choo" trains.

When Grandpa meets God, I hope he takes me with him to Heaven. I can hardly wait to hear the questions Grandpa will be asking. God and Grandpa will talk about the beauty of the world and the spectacular views from above. They will share thoughts on justice and making the world a better place for humanity to live. Most of all God will lay his hand on Grandpa's head and grant him peace and freedom from pain in his new life.

He always was lucky enough to have a job. In addition, not any job. He had a job flying airplanes. He loved his job. He did not write much but he did write one poem about his work. AJ, I hope that whatever work you choose in life that you like it as much as Grandpa liked his job of flying airplanes.

AJ, think carefully about what you want to do; then go after it with the same gusto that Grandpa went after learning how to be a great pilot. Enjoy what he wrote about his office. I know God has a place for Grandpa in Heaven because he walked though life trying to do what was right for everyone who touched his life. Your Grandpa was a man of tolerance and patience when it came to the pain in his back. He was a man's man as he did not complain.

AJ, you get your love of art in part from your Grandpa who appreciated all the beauty he saw. AJ, I asked your Grandpa if I could include the poem he wrote in this collection of thoughts. He gave me permission, savor it, and read it slowly for it is so beautiful.

Grandpa Flying High in the Sky

Sandie Barrie

"LUCKY GUY"

FROM MY OFFICE SEAT
I HAVE SEEN A SUNRISE
  AND SUNSET BEYOND DESCRIPTION
I HAVE SEEN THE KNIFE EDGE OF THE SIERRAS
  AND THE BROAD BACK OF THE ROCKIES
I HAVE SEEN THE PACIFIC, THE ATLANTIC
  AND IN BETWEEN THE MIGHTY MISSISSIPPI
I HAVE SEEN TOO MANY SMALL LAKES TO REMEMBER
  AND ALL THE LAKES THAT THEY CALL GREAT

FROM MY OFFICE SEAT
I HAVE SEEN THE MAJESTIC CITIES
  AND IN BETWEEN THE WIDE OPEN SPACES
I HAVE SEEN THE FIELDS OF CROPS
  AND DESERTS OF SAND
I HAVE SEEN THE FOREST OF PINES
  AND THE CACTUS OF THE SOUTHWEST
I HAVE SEEN THE ENDLESS INTERSTATES
  AND ROADS JUST MADE OF DIRT

FROM MY OFFICE SEAT
I HAVE SEEN THE HOMES OF PEOPLE
  BOTH RICH AND POOR
I HAVE SEEN THE ELEGANCE OF A DESERT NIGHT
  AND THE ENDLESS LIGHTS OF THE BIG CITIES
I HAVE SEEN A WHITE PUFFY CLOUD BECOME
  A THUNDERSTORM REACHING TO THE HEAVENS
I HAVE SEEN OTHER AIRPLANES LEAVE THEIR TRAILS
  FOR OTHERS AND ME TO FOLLOW

FROM MY OFFICE SEAT
I HAVE SEEN THE EARTH IN ITS PALE GREEN OF SPRING
  ITS MULTI-COLORS OF SUMMER
HER COUNTLESS TANS AND GOLD OF FALL
  AND FINALLY DRESSED IN WHITE FOR WINTER

FROM MY OFFICE SEAT I HAVE SEEN

AJ, I always liked to write. I wrote the following for your Grandpa many years ago. Then on a Christmas Eve a few years back, your Dad read it to him for me. You will see it in Grandpa's bathroom. That is where your Grandpa chose to put it, where he and everyone who came to our house could see.

Ego Amo Te

sharing...sharing...sharing

I am glad that you knew from the beginning...

That you are I would marry! And a marriage it has been... commingling our lives, even more our very beings... and yet each of us is so different . . .

You with your airplanes and me with my sewing; you with your need to be alone and me with my need to be with others; you with your work and me with my homework . . .

Both of us know it will take death to part us and so there is no need for jealousy or competition or fear. It is just there the realization that this relationship is on forever . . .

And the relationship has fostered growth in both of us, as one toddles forth in a new venture, the other one is tugged along and together, but separately we struggle and the success of one, spurs on the success of the other.

Knowing growth brings life is fundamental . . . we spend a lot of time watering and sunning each other... allowing the little buds of difference to exist and changing . . . sometimes each other but mostly ourselves.

We renew our commitment to our relationship over and over: sometimes once a day, sometimes once a month, sometimes once a year. Renewing our relationship over and over with time has brought great peace and beauty to each and both of us as we touch . . .

And so I am glad you knew, almost from the beginning that you and I would marry . . .

Sandie, Circa 1996

72

AJ, someday you will know who the person that you want to spend your life with is. I hope that when you say I do, it will be forever!

AJ, every Mom should be so lucky to have three sons. I wanted children right away when I got married.

I wrote the following many many years ago when I was first going to write a book before I even dreamed I could be so blessed to have a Grandson, like you.

Sandie Barrie

Freddie

My first son
blue eye, blond hair . . .
with him I learned
all over again, what
it was like to crawl, and
climb and walk.

Seeing with him the
newness in a flower, the
freedom of a butterfly,
the softness of snow and
his quiet sensitivity to
life has taught me not
to make promises I couldn't
keep.

Soon taller than me, he will
be and yet it was such a
short time ago I sat in our
first home, holding him
in my arms . . . rocking him
to sleep.

Reading and spelling, slowly
and writing over and over . . . he
learned so many things I once
knew and had forgotten.

The beauty of a child growing
and getting to watch the process.

Oh what a gift from the One above.

Kevin

My second son,

Smiling and dimple faced . . .

has been a delight,

Although stubborn

he can be.

Close he came behind his

brother and my hands were

filled. And yet the two

of them had each other,

and I watched them interact.

Wondering just when the

little one would be just

big enough to slug the

other one . . . just once.

He has taught me to

listen for he talks faster

than I and yet clearly he

states what it is that is

on his mind.

And yes, he has grown, but

not so tall that I can't

look him in the eye.

And say . . . I'll

try harder, how about you?

For you see he and I are

so much alike . . .

Christopher

My third son, a cutie weighing

in at 9.2 . . . Is growing like a

weed soon to be in school all

day, it doesn't seem possible.

And, the first words he said were

"I love you", and even today our

favorite game is to see who can

sing these words the loudest . . .

Peanut butter and jelly sandwiches

and lots of water, cold water are

his favorite foods. And yet he has

always liked his bananas, apples, and

oranges.

Projects and his friends fill his

day. And each night along with his

brothers, he wants to say the

Our Father and be tucked in . . .

Circa 1979

Freddie, Your Dad

Freddie, your Dad, is my oldest son. He was born to me when I was 21. As a young boy, he was shy and quiet. He never learned how to fight. I remember that his kindergarten teacher predicted that he would be an engineer. I wish I could find her and tell her she was right, he is a software engineer. AJ, you can really look up to your father. He is gentle, kind, and patient. I know that you will be able to remember the hours he spent reading to you and cooking the evening meals. You liked the Lemon Chicken and the cookies.

Your father invented VERONICA. It was a software program on the Internet. It was popular and he helped a lot of people that never knew about the hours that he spent running the computers so that they could look up things. He is very unpretentious. He solved computer-programming problems and rarely talked about his stellar solutions. He simply knew that he made a difference and that was enough for him.

The one thing that I will always respect your father for was his decision not to take the high paying job. He changed jobs but when the employer wanted all his time, he recognized that would have huge implications on you. He decided that he wanted to be a father and that being a father was more important than being a high paid employee or entrepreneur. He simply preferred being a Dad, your Dad who was present to you. It was not a hard choice for him. He was truly happy making sure that you had his time not his money.

As the choices between family and work have to be dealt with, I hope that you will be able to remember all the hours that your Dad spent with you. I hope that you will find the choices that you need to make to be easy decisions, decisions made because they are right for you and the ones you love.

AJ, when your Dad goes to Heaven, you will know that he is welcomed by God because he took the time to be with family . . . with your Mom, and your sister, and you! God will reward him with a big computer that will work perfectly as he plays his video games and checks on the latest Reno Aces baseball scores.

Uncle Kevin

Uncle Kevin came along when I was 22. He grew fast and at age two was about the same size of your father. Uncle Kevin and your dad played easily together, enjoying the red fire engines given to them by a childless military couple when we lived in the trailer in Atchison, KS.

Uncle Kevin grew up fast and went to work after I forged his birth certificate so he could get a job. He worked at fast food places for many years before he started to work at an early age in a warehouse.

AJ, Uncle Kevin liked to spend time with you when you were very young and he loved giving you candy and pop. Uncle Kevin waited a long time to find the right lady and he married and with her they had three little girls, who always looked up to you.

Uncle Kevin worked hard to provide for his family, he spent hours of time finishing his house, making a beautiful backyard for his children, and keeping track of many details as he threaded together a beautiful life for his family.

Uncle Kevin is a man of principles. While he follows the rules, he does take time to have fun. The little dimples he had as a young boy remained with him all the days of his life. From Uncle Kevin you can learn to share your smile often for anyone that sees his smile knows that life is okay and that whatever is going on in life will be alright.

AJ, when Uncle Kevin goes to Heaven, he also will be welcomed by God because He took the time to be with family . . . his wife and his three little girls! God will reward him with a big TV screen that works perfectly where he can watch the Bears and the Cubs play.

Uncle Chris

Uncle Chris came along when I was 28. Uncle Chris liked sports and played baseball a lot. Along the way he also learned how to play golf.

Uncle Chris had many friends when he was in high school. The house phone was always ringing.

I remember the night we got a call and jumped out of bed. We ran to the detention center looking for Chris, only to find he was not there. I started to call our home and the phone recorder kept coming on, until finally Uncle Chris answered. Grandpa and I had not realized that Uncle Chris was in his bed when we received the prank call.

Uncle Chris was on the basketball team and his nickname was "Raspberry". I use to love to go to the games in the Sparks High gym and have everyone screaming out his name anticipating he would hit the basket.

Uncle Chris was happy, he enjoyed life. He liked adventure and he always kept his word. He made friends easily with his wide smile and his quick ability to connect his conversation with anyone that came along his way.

I remember Chris's 21st birthday when he brought home a dog, he named the dog Bear Bear. Bear Bear taught Chris about responsibility.

Uncle Chris left Sparks and moved to Portland where he

forged a new life for himself.

Bear Bear Not Wanting to Leave Grandma's House

Uncle Chris loved the outdoors and hiked everywhere. He worked in hotels and bars and eventually got the ideal job in the art museum.

AJ, when Uncle Chris goes to Heaven, he will be welcomed by God because He took the time to be with family and friends. He never forgot the people that helped him out when he first moved to Portland.

God will reward him with a big fancy golf course where he will be able to play for as many holes as he desires. Then he will go into watch his TV screen that works perfectly and he will watch the Bears and the Cubs play.

AJ, my hope is that you will always treat your Mom like your Dad and his brothers have treated me. I have always been treated with respect, kindness, and gentleness.

Your Grandpa and I are proud of our three sons. Blessing your Mom is a family tradition, started many years ago by your Great Grandpa, carried on by your Grandpa, and your Dad and his brothers - a tradition I know that you will want to carry forward to the next generation. Love your Mom always!

AJ

I wrote many years ago the following passage. I found it as I was cleaning out all the old papers and preparing to write this book and another one about my nursing career.

Here is what I wrote many years ago and it still stands today uncut from my first writing.

The hope of my life lies in my three sons. As any mother, I want for them the best. And, that does not mean I want fancy cars, fancy homes with their mortgages, or the other soft things of life. I want for them, for each of them the need to help someone. Helping others is the central theme, which has invaded Fred and my life. I want Freddie, Kevin, and Chris to be able to appreciate this aspect of life. Helping doesn't mean doing everything or giving up everything for another. It does mean sharing, sharing your talents for keeping God given talents to one's self is stifling.

Having the confidence of intact self-esteem is central in the process of helping. For when the self-esteem is whole, the knocks in life are not so hard or devastating. It is important to know how to pick one's self up and to move forward. Having confidence in seeing those issues that need to be dealt with, whether it is the poor attitude in an individual or a large helping project for many individuals brings forth the flower from the bloom. Having the ability to share your smiles and allowing your eyes to glow with those that you meet is central to life.

AJ, I started to write this collection of thoughts when you were four and I finally finished it when you were twelve, I sincerely wanted you to know the men that I have written about in this book.

AJ, you have taught me many things in your young life.

You have taught me how to enjoy the things that I like doing, like writing and sewing . . . and starting to draw and paint. You have taught me how to listen carefully to what you say. You have taught me how to be a Grandma.

AJ, I have truly enjoyed watching you draw, I hope you continue to enjoy drawing for the rest of your life. I hope that you remember each time you put pencil to paper that God has given you a truly unique gift that you can choose to share with others. I enjoy hanging your pictures on our refrigerator, I enjoy getting the Christmas gifts of pictures you drew and painted. Keep it up, someday you will draw something that will help a lot of people. I will be watching and smiling when that day happens.

I hope that as you grow you will develop into a man that enables the virtues discussed in this book. It is hard to sum it up, but these men are men of service. They are all very manly and yet there is something soft and cozy about each one of them. They have learned many hard lessons over the years. And, they have taught me many lessons, I am a better person because I got to know each one of these men.

Some of them went to war and some of them fought not to go. Some of them had only one job and some of them had many jobs. Some of them are educated and some of them are not. Some of them are alive and some of them are not. But, AJ they all are at peace with themselves knowing that they have done the best they could with what God has given them.

I know each one of them would tell you to work hard, to play hard, to have fun, and to enjoy your journey on the way to Heaven.

AJ, enjoy life on your way to Heaven!

Your Birthday Present

AJ, please keep this book and on your birthday read it each year. If you ever have a son be sure to share it with him. And, when life gets tough take the time to read this book. And, when life is happy, remember that your Grandma really had a fun time writing this for you.

I hope you read this book often!

Hope you remember these men. They are everything I wanted the men in my life to be. Every woman should be so lucky! They are compassionate, peaceful, gentle, comfortable, generous, helping, patient, calm, and humble. They are all men of integrity.

They bring stability to a changing world. It is easy to see God is in our world because you only need to look into the eyes of these men to see Him.

Walk through life in peace because God is with you!

Love, Grandma 2010

www.ingramcontent.com/pod-product-compliance
Lightning Source LLC
Chambersburg PA
CBHW072207090426
42740CB00012B/2425